SHATTERED

SHATTERED

TERRY HAUPTMAN

North Star Press
www.NorthStarPress.com
Since 1969

ISBN: 978-1-68201-166-9

North Star Press of St. Cloud Inc.
www.NorthStarPress.com

First Edition

Type set in Brioso Pro and FLW Exhibition.

Printed in the United States of America.

Interior images and cover photo by Terry Hauptman.

Book design by Liz Dwyer, with love.

OTHER POETRY BOOKS BY TERRY HAUPTMAN:

Masquerading In Clover: Fantasy of The Leafy Fool
  Boston: Four Zoas, 1980
  (With hand-painted plates.)

Rattle
  Cardinal Press, Tulsa, OK: 1982
  (With an introduction by Meridel LeSeuer)

On Hearing Thunder
  North Star Press, St. Cloud, MN: 2004.
      (With color plates)

The Indwelling of Dissonance
  North Star Press, St. Cloud, MN: 2016.

The Tremulous Seasons
  North Star Press, St. Cloud, MN: 2019.

Rubies In The Mud
  Polaris Publications, An Imprint of North Star Press, 2020.

Fallen Angels
  North Star Press, St. Cloud Minnesota, 2022.

PRAISE

The poems are on fire, on fire with grief and anger, as they should be. In *Shattered*, Terry Hauptman utters a collective wail, a lamentation, and a cry of rage. Collective, because she creates choruses with Lorca, Neruda, Thelonius Monk, Joy Harjo, Yehuda Halevi (and many others), leaping across cultures and languages. Yet the voice in these chants is distinctly Hauptman's own: ecstatic, full-throated. She sings the Blackmoon, the Bloodmoon; she conjures a hyacinth fire of tears; she mourns and curses, and calls for peace in calamitous times. "We are a country/ at war with itself," she rightly declares in this book that appears in the throes of that war.

-Rosanna Warren

"Terry is a rare talent of poet and performer. Her work is incantatory, rhapsodic, with themes of feminist Jewish mysticism, braided with prayer and ceremony. She is also a prolific painter of enormous allegorical scrolls, reminiscent of William Blake and ancient tapestry. She creates a passionate narrative particularly rooted in Jewish ritual and song. Terry's work as a poet, and performer, often resonates with drums that shake the house, a sagacious and multicultural hip hop.

-Annice Jacoby
Street Art San Francisco, Mission Muralismo

Terry's work has made a transition to the highest level of respect. I have always supported her work as a poet and artist and enjoyed many years of friendship. We inspire each other and connect on many spiritual journeys. My eyes are open wide. I'm taking in the beauty and at the same time feeling how lucky I am to know so well the vision from which it came. She weaves her hands over the canvas, and creates magical beauty.

-Frank Anthony, Master painter

"When I opened Terry Hauptman's volume *Fallen Angels*, the power of her shamanic voice took me to the depths, parted their "blood ribbons" and shrouded me in "the burnt lilac dust, in the solitude of ash," In every epigraph and dedication are beloveds alive and dead. These poems are the essence of what poetry is in the darkest times: Poetry is the lamp, the ember, the torch re-lit, the star guiding us back to the light of ourselves.

Fallen Angels bears the truth of tragedy, the desecration of life created by humans; their own and our earth, but Terry Hauptman also delivers the love, the beauty, the ecstasy humanity also gives unreservedly, because she writes these lines in a balance harvested from her own life experiences. The Fallen Angel mixed-media scrolls providing the defiantly radiant cover and section breaks, are crossroads that beckon us to find our new ways to be in this world. These are poems that sing, chant, invoke, and howl incantations:

> Pulse-beat
> Of the dissonant
>
> The inner sanctum
> Rising within you
> Free your spirit of hope
>
> *Canto Jondo*
> For Gerald McBride

It is a wild ride, linking arms and clasping hands with these Fallen Angels! The poems reach into the abyss, and come out "Bearing Witness to the cordillera winds of stars/ put out in the burning rain." The Pandemic Time has changed us. Terry Hauptman's poetry and art gives us our changes with open hands and many languages: Bedouin palms, and Mizrahi songs" "ancient piyyuts and jazz. With colors and shapes, we find maps of ourselves shimmering in. She offers us choices to midwife, more change, and the indefatigable, courageous companionship of her Fallen Angels."

-Reverend Claire Longtin North
Ministry in the Mountains,
Manchester, Vermont

Terry Hauptman…
"Visionary Calibanista"
-Larry Smith
Editor of CALIBAN

"Terry Hauptman's poetry is high art"
-Joel Weishaus, Poet

SHATTERED

I dreamed a revolution
Away from evil

Odysseus Elytis

Tell me how you lived your dream
In some place
And I'll tell you who you are

-Fady Joudah

DEDICATION

For Bob and Kira,
My Beloved family and friends
Whose soul-alchemy inspires my becoming

In the firelight of *Duende's* song
In the dark night of luminous dreams

For Silver and Mahalla.

Thank you Liz Dwyer for
the beautiful book design.

Thank you Curtis Dwyer.

And for Eartha Redwing.

CONTENTS

KIRA'S SONG

These are the winds
   That carry us stargazing with owls in the forest.
     These are the winds that carry us through
       The dark, the light
         The everyday care
           Calling down the spirit-fires
             Through cadmium clouds.

These are the winds that sanctify
   Our blessing and songs

Daughter of salt and pines,

These are the winds
   That carry us through
     The hard stories,
       The roosting of crows,
         The hoop of rain and flowers

Your black-tourmaline
   Earth luminosity
     Shines through
       Your compassionate heart

Calling you to me
   Calling me to you
     Daughter

<u>INCANTATIONS:</u>

SONGS FROM AFAR

AND THE NEWLY DEPARTED

And the day came
When the risk it took to remain
Tightly closed in the bud
Was more painful
Than the risk it took to bloom,
This is the Element of Freedom
                              -Alicia Keyes

Did it hurt my brother
When I said I saw angels in the house
Playing with the wolf?
                    -Mahmoud Darwish

To the eye of the spiral
We fly
From the luminous fires of life,
We return.
                    - Terry Hauptman

ON HEARING THUNDER

For Wahru

Blues riffs strut moon black
I listen to her talk spirit
O yeah move mountains on nightstreets
Stoop woman of ancestral memory
           drumming
'I've got to deal with this'
'I'm just coming to myself'
'The wings beat at my feet
So I pick a night and I dance.'

    The moon rubs her back on the black keys
    I Listen to her talk spirit
    Talk story. Talk ninth street
    Be ninth street   Talk energies
    Night birds cawing
    Like this beautiful woman who plays the piano
    And looks like Ida Lupino.

The occult ache of her rage
O yeah totemic
Dreams inside the wind
She shakes out the demons
Shakes her whole arms
Shakes the demons out from her fingers
Stands crazy in broom weed
Shaking out silver snakes
Head pressed to her warrior heart
In the afterglow of fireweed
Summons the luminous dark
Shakes out the demons
Shakes her whole arms

Blues riffs strut moon black
Stunned by her own music.

I see her coming towards me
Like Harriet Tubman warming to danger
Her belly voice emphatic as jalapeño peppers
Summons the laughing dark.
This quasar moves with a purpose
She is this Baaad.
Blues riffs strut moon black
Wild-eyed like memory
In the moonlight.

WAHRU'S SONG:
A FORCE TO BE RECKONED WITH

For Wahru Cleveland
(April 1,1945-November 13, 2022)

Sunlight returns
  Licking scarlet
    From mountain tears

Our friendship rooted in your friendship
  Our souls rooted in your soul,
    Our hearts rooted in your heart
      Our stories rooted in your story,
        Our mysteries rooted in your mystery
        Our song rooted in your song

Rest in Peace, Wahru
Rest in Peace

AT THE VERY END
OF YOUR LIFE ON EARTH

To The Memory of Wahru

*One fine morning, when this world
is over, I'll fly away.
To that land on dark celestial shores,
I'll fly away, fly away*
- Carolyn Hester

I sing just to know that I'm alive
-Nina Simone

At the very end of your life on earth
  Your white table cloth over
    A Dell City picnic table
    Rolled out,
      With fried okra, wine, and cheese
        Pot liquor and sugar skulls
          With Day of The Dead marigolds,
            Añil de Muerto,
            And broomweed
              Under a golden sun.

Sistah Ngoma circling your
  Djembe beat,
    Ashiko Congos, Congas,
    Rhythmically sounding
    Your dance of life

    "I've got a right to walk these streets,
      Walk 'em in the night,
      And anytime I want to
      I've got a right to walk these streets
        Fight back!

Throughout Oklahoma and Ohio,
  So loved
    At the Herland Collective
    "Just this Bad"
      At the Paris Flea Market,

The Winds of Tiger Mountain
  Falling forward
    With Safiya Henderson Holmes
    In Harlem,
      "Peace Y'all,
        Call it"
And with Kira chanting,
  "What do we want?"
    "Health care,"
      "When do we want it?"
        "Now."

Your gap-tooth smile,
  High cheekbones,
    Drumming with Joyce,
      At the break of day.

        Grief
          Becoming
            Wind

        Wind
          Becoming
            Song

TALKING ALL NIGHT THUNDER
For Wahru

Talking all night thunder
  In spidery winds,
    Praising talking drum spirits
      In the lightning's wing.

You cut your milk teeth on Santana
  Driving your car
    Boogie Blue
      Though the green winds of your departure
        Invoking ancestral spirits

Your butterfly dreams
  The burnt wings of story,
    Crushed
      In the palm of your hand.

Listening to Sweet Honey In The Rock,
  As we lose you
    Forever
      Sistah Ngoma following you,
        Your faith, your love.

REMEMBER

Even the most broken life
Can be restored to its moments.
-Carolyn Forche

For those who stir the pots
   In the World Central Kitchen in Kyiv,

      Kissing the fallen petals
         Of their hearts,
            The spiral roots
               Of the earth,

Crying for what remains
   In shattered winds,
      The bombed-out shelters
         Of broken lives
            The soot of lullabies.

José Andrés from
   World Central Kitchen
      Feeds the hungry in Kyiv, Ukraine,

Añil del Muerto sunflowers
   Wounded in mud and death
      Bend, bringing hope
         Towards
            The shattered sky,

As dark smoke circles murdered children,
   Crows, picking on corpses,
      Flee the night's
         Sunflowers of the dead's
            Mass graves in Mariupal.

We weep for the dead and the living
  As the great violinists of Odessa
    Shatter tears
      In sheltered rooms
        Before leaving for Poland
          At dawn,
            Where their ancestors died
              In Auschwitz ovens
                Humming a prayer.

Listening to the dead
  And the living,
    We hear our Beloved Paul Robeson sing,
      "The Night of The Murdered Poets,"
        For the Yiddish Poets
          Falsely accused of espionage,
            Murdered by Stalin,
              Murdered in the Soviet Union in 1952.

Remembering my grandparents'
  Workman's Circle grief,
    In the deep rivering night.

"The Night of the Murdered Poets,"
  The Night of the Murdered Yiddish Poets,
    Paul Robeson singing in Yiddish,
      'Never say that you're going
        Your last way,'
          "You nit Keynmol
            Partisan Song"
              "Partizaner"

Robeson singing the Holocaust era
   Partisan song,
      In solidarity with the Jewish People.
         Breaking the vessels
            In the deep rivering night.

Why are we teaching our children
   To forget this cry?

Are we teaching our children to forget this cry for unity
   And prayer?

NO PEACE IN THE DOLOR
AND DEVASTATION OF WAR:
THE DISASTERS OF WAR

War shatters the Kyiv night
  The arc of love,
    Shatters the mineral dark,
     Democracy's heart
      Ukraine's Blackmoon
       Bloodmoon
        Over balconies' dust,
         The blueing of death
         On mass graves,

Broken glass infernos
  Of weeping besieged

Russia bombing The Holocaust Museum
  At Babyn Yar
    Memorializing
     The death of thousands
      Of Roma and Jews

As Black and Brown foreign students
  Fleeing Ukraine
    Face Racism
     At the border

The world screams
  No to autocracy
    No to war!

Listen to the deep music
  Of falling violins,

Children dying in weeping winds'
  Heartbreaking brutality
    As Ukraine defends herself
    In the gunpowder night.

Ukrainian refugees
  Exiled under Poland's sky
    Women and children sparking
      Dark wounds of destiny's cries
        Shadowing freedom
          In the arc of prayer.

Songbirds unmask the face of death
  The heart of the wounded
    Descending on twilight's stairs.

Bees circle earth-roots
  Rubbing funeral oils
    On the forehead of the missing
      In the shadow-world of care.

We are a country
  At war with itself,
    At war with freedom.

Fifty years after the war
  You find your house
    On the outskirts of Auschwitz
      Near the crematorium
        And knock on the door.
          "This was my home before the war"
            "We have your grandmother's sewing machine,
              Do you want to take it back."

"HERE AND THERE,
A BLEEDING SUN,
SHINES EACH DAY."

—Jorge Somariba, Nicaraguan Mural Painter, Guest artist in Norman, Oklahoma

No hay capacious más ancho
que el dolor
No hay universo como aquel que sangra

There is no space wider than
That of grief,
There is no universe like that which bleeds.
-Pablo Neruda

Neruda's cobalt blue
  Cordillera tears of grief
   Spill over the earth's
    Bread of love

    For the blood
      That ran in the streets
        In the condor's night wind,

       "Hablad por mis palabras
          Por mi sangre"

        "Speak through my words
           And through my blood."
World-weary
  In the terror of volcanos,
   The torpor of death,
    Poisoned by The Junta,
     The Chilean military,
      You had opposed,
       Discordant
         In The Tree of Life.

CORDOBA'S SONG

For Federico Garcia Lorca
(1898-1936)

> *Where do the dreams go?*
> *Born of faith and illusion*
> *where there's no road*
> *And no footprints*
> *-Lorca*

> *Green, how much I love you green,*
> *green-wind, green boughs,*
> *ship on the sea,*
> *horse on the mountain.*
> *-Lorca*

Lorca's lost honey of Grenada
  Rivering *duende's* pulse,
    Gypsy ballads thundering
      Al-Hambra of Andalusian dreams
        Swimming in the shadows of hope.

Romance of guitars,
  Laughing in the *cante jondo*
    Black sounds
      Deepening death songs
      At dawn

Albe of morning light
  Lilacs in the pink sun
    The strawberry moon

Gacela's of unexpected love
  Black roses of Cordoba
    Qasidas of doves,

Summer's sulfur of pink honey
  And blue-eyed grass,
    Dirt-candy
      In the blue mud's
        Wild soul.

Lorca's Grenada,
  Qasida of the dark sky's
    Endless love,
      Cantos of forever
        Burning in broken glass
          Reaching the sun.

Cry of Cordoba
  Through the olive trees,
    "*Verde, que te quiero verde*"
      Green, how I love you, green."

Hummingbirds dreaming cries of doves,
  Shot by the fascists,
    Gacela of the dark death,
      Gacela of unexpected love.

Nightbirds listening to the love-fire
  Rising up
    Into the break of day
      Into the deepening sun.

The full moon's mountain-river
  Balancing stones
    Cries for change
      In the telluric dark
        Fluting the bones.

SINGING FOR JUSTICE, FOREVER

For Dan Carr (1951- 2012)
And for Julia Ferrari

Snow drifted through the wooden slats
  Of the funeral parlor building
    Converted to a letterpress studio
      Where Four Zoas Golgonooza Press
        Resided.

I printed my first letterpress
  "For The Children of Atlanta" broadside
    Here, where our visions for Justice
      Blossomed together in song.

Today Tyre Nichols was bludgeoned to death
  By police, in the Memphis heat.

  "Trouble, oh trouble,
    Come sing these blues away'

We must fight this Hate
  With our hearts and souls,
    Crying out to Dan and Julia
      Singing Mercy's song,
        At the break of day.

KADDISH FOR LEONORA
My Mother (1925-2018)

When I saw your soul's light across the sky.
  With your spirit smiling at your burial,

I knew
  That we would walk with you,
    Eternally,
      As the hyacinth fire of tears
        Spilled down our faces,
          As the violet shadows of the heart
            Broke into the mystery.
              Spilling tears into the dirt
                Shoveled over your coffin.

  As the sun blessed
    All of us with love,
      Leonora,
        Our mother of beauty and joy.

ANCESTRAL

"Yiddisha Nightingale
Sing me a song"
-Maurice Burkhardt, 1911

"Grandma Lillie… what is the secret of your 100 years?"
"Stale bread and pickle juice."

Kvelling with pride
  For your grandchildren
    Singing
      "Schnapps is schnapps
        But poetry is poetry"

Forgetting your journey
  From Minsk-Gibernia to New York,

Never to return to Russia's pogroms,
  Never wanting to return,
    Telling the story of your baby brother's death,
      Punching holes in a cardboard box,
        And throwing him overboard,
          In the starry night
            Winds of sorrow.

Eating the last piece of bread
  Fighting for the label,
    The heel,
      The *kvatch*

Listening to my mother and my grandmother
  Speaking Yiddish
    Winding the red thread
      At the kitchen table.
        Watching the stars,
          Rising to joy.
            Celebrating our family's love.

Dancing to "Come on a my house,
  My house a come on,"
    "I'm going cocoa loco in my cocoa."
Watching the weeping moon
  Lighting up Shaddai's ankle bracelet,
    Telling stories,
      Dreaming a different ending.

Asking why
  Louis Armstrong,
    King of Queens, New York,
      Wore a Jewish star
        Through the dark
          Corona Streets?

My grandma telling me
  Her gratitude
    That an immigrant Jewish family
      Helped him buy his first horn.

These are the stories
  We never hear
    That bind our unity
      Together.

THE GHOST SHIPS OF KIPTOPEKE
On Virginia's Eastern Shore

Home to pelicans and gulls,
 Birds nest in the abandoned
  Ghost ships of Kiptopeke,
   Marooned from World War II,
    One ship storming
     The allied invasion of Normandy

Now forming an offshore breakwater
 Blocking the ocean's power
  Near the mouth of The Chesapeake Bay,
   The concrete ghost ships
    Of Koptopeke's "Big water"
     Casting a blue-black shadow
      As twilight,
       Haunted by history,
        Moves towards us.

Let the winds
 Carry us
  As we dance in the
   Silver sandbars'
    Textural dark,

Leaves veining crimson,
 In Virginia
  As the ghost ships of Kiptopeke
   Disappear.

FIRST LANDING STATE PARK,

Cape Henry, North Virginia Beach *

Crossing the wooden bridge
  To the beach's bay,
    What treachery these navigated shores,
      Bringing slaves to Virginia's plantations,
        A memory of torture's slaveships
          Piercing through.

We were waiting for horses
  To rise up out of the water
    Whinnying at daybreak

Riding in between the waves,
  Not knowing where to emerge,
    Splashing around the sun,
      Hearing the strength of Freedom's Song.

At Don Valerios Mexican restaurant
  In Cape Charles Virginia,
    We witness freedom's
      Blood Memory
        Remembering Slavery's dead

Calling down the spirits
  From the gallows cries,
    The sorrow songs
      In the blood winds of lullabies.

We were waiting for the horses
  To rise up out of the water
    As we wade in the river

      Of fear and hope.

*A National Natural landmark built by African-American Civilian Conservation Corps engineers 1933-1940.

ALTIPLANO
*For Rigoberta Menchu**

> *The silenced majority*
> *that same day*
> *will decide*
> *which small piece of the sky*
> *belongs to them…*
> *-Rigoberta Menchu*

Mayan Indian of the Altiplano,
  Quiche, fighting for your Guatemalan people
    Lost in struggle's transformative power,
      Fighting for justice,
        Marking the Mayan Calendar of Days,
          Embracing *Quetzalcoatl's* indigenous soul
            Growing up impoverished
              In the fincas' ancestral pulse
                Where the world holds your hope,

Planting maize
  In the heart of the earth,
    Breathe of the Altiplano
      Picking coffee
        Where the universe
          Bears your love

Planting Nahuatl seeds
  Before your peasant march,
    Burning copal
      Chanting
        Songs for the earth's poor,
          From the hive of miracles,
            The underbelly of doves,

Witnessing the sacred days
  Of the harvest's sun,
    Guatemala,
      The breath of freedom's home,
        Teaching us the new moon of beginnings,
          The soul as a guide to freedom's song.

*Rigoberta Menchu, author of *I, Rigoberta Menchu,* was awarded The Nobel Peace Prize in 1992.

SALT WINDS

Ocean birds
  Burn through the waves'
    Earth source of life

Wind and fire
  Bleed through
    Salt winds
      Shattering song

Two weeks traveling,
  Teaches me my own vulnerability,
    Breaking my spirit
      With a soulful cry

Teaching me
  Again and again,
    The rhythms of unpredictable life.
      Even the mountains
        Shape-shift
          Welcoming me home,

          Wash sadness away
           In the thunders open palm.

SONG

What was I looking for
  In the music of winds
    In the arc of mountains
      In the blood winds of freedom's song?

And the song is for freedom
  And the song is for love
    And the song's in the night winds
      Dark winds, firmaments

And the song it is joyful
  And the song it is bold
    And the song is forgotten
      In the violent winds.

Get yourself moving
  Through the waters,
Get yourself moving
  Through the void,
Get your self moving,
  Through muddy waters,
Get yourself moving,
  Journey on.

And the cry is for Freedom
  And the cry is for Love
    And the cry's in the
      Night winds
        Dark winds, firmaments.

And the cry
  It is empty
    And the cry it is bold,
      And the cry is forgotten
        In the violent void.

SONG FOR DERORA BERNSTEIN
(1942-1973)

You are gone
You have left us in the night.
I'm alone,
I can hear your voice turning,

You are gone,
You have left us in the night,
I'm alone,
I can hear your voice turning,

And turning,
  And turning,
   I'm alone,
     I can hear your voice turning.

KOHOUTEK

And the solar wind blows dust
  From head to tail,
    And particles whirling in intrigue strike
      Flint with fire
        Flint with fire

As the starlight
  That strikes the comet's veil
    Inquires
      Will the rivers of Apheta run dry?
        Will the rivers of Apheta run dry?

ECLIPSE

On the path of totality
    As the moon crosses
        In front of the sun,
The black eyelids of the
    Solar Corona
        Circling the eclipsing moon
            Engulf the moon's shadow life
                As black resins of the diamond ring
                    Scorch the mineral dark.

We augur the final red spark
    Flying like a bird
        Waiting for the same sun
            To shine again.

ISLETA PUEBLO

For Elena Carr and Federico Abeita

The Irish Priest says Mass at
  Isleta Pueblo
    Before Federico dances
      The Black Eye Dance

Telling me of
  The zig zag Lightning Dance
    That brought down the rain
      To the Rio Grande Valley
        Where the Manzano Mountains
        Reign.

Black clouds and scarlet sage
  Over desert-star
    Hearts of the tribe.

VORTEX

The angels eyelashes white from trauma
   Flutter on the dharmic wheel of chance,
     Listening with adoration
      To the cerulean winds of dance.

Male turtles flip other male turtles
   On their backs
     Competing for female love,
      Children flip them back right-side up
       Chanting "Peace be with you,"
        Listening to the squeaks of hawks and doves.

NIGHT MUSIC

We lose our way
  In the honey
    Of the forest's blue clay
      As fireflies spark deer
     In the clearing.

Who are we following hornets
  To their nests
    Flirting with doves?

We lose our way
  In the honey
    Of the forest's blue clay

Rubbing funeral oil on crows
  As the winds of misfortune
    Thunder with love.

35

HAUNTED BY DREAMS:

TREE OF LIFE

*For the soul is a wanderer with many
hands and feet*
-Joy Harjo

*A crystal of willow, a poplar of water,
a tall fountain the wind arches over,
a tree deeply rooted yet dazzling,
a course of a river that turns, moves on
forever arriving.*
- Octavio Paz

SOMETIMES

For Carol Heffer

Sometimes
   Rivering the memory of you
      Traveling in Morocco,
         Sleeping on the beach,
            Waking to a circle of men
               Surrounding you

Between worlds
   Fleeing to safety
      Swimming in the shadows of sand.

In Tunisia,
   Asking questions
      Hidden in the dream of fire,
         The music of time,

Let us walk together as friends,
   Under the wolf-whelping moon ,
      The heartbeat of winds,
         Night and day
            Under the sun,
               Dreaming companions music.

Asking questions,
   As the tide rolls in,
      Weaving winds of love,

Listening to the harmonies
   Of songbirds in the pines,
      The sunlight drenched in sweet decay
         Where blue dragonflies flame,
            Resplendent in burning winds.

Black butterflies
Dance towards love,
Listening to the music
Of crows and doves.

BLESSINGS: HEALING HANDS WILL TRAVEL

For Roz Richards

Listening to your horn of the moon prayer,
  Lost in dreams
    Incandescent in grief,

Watching the blood moon's
  Obsidian night
    In its struggle
      Against the tides

I should have known
  Your smoke-prayer
    From the palm of
      Your healing hands
        Would set me on fire
        With your beauty.

HAUNTED BY WINDS:
WALK IN BEAUTY
For Bob

At eighty
  Your deep forest walks
    On dirt roads
      Whirl with joy
        In the honeysuckle winds,
          The balsam fires,
            The I-Thou of doves,
              The cries of love.

MOUNTAIN TOWER MEMORY
IN THE MOUNTAINS, THERE YOU FEEL FREE.

For Malonta and Don Hugo

Mapping winds through earth-songs,
　Changing direction on Manicknung,
　　Sacred mountain,
　　　Walking the fire-tower trail,
　　　　Wandering with stories
　　　　　In the deep-forest's green
　　　　　　Rhythms of change,

At Café Oudry,
　Telling stories of mountain hikers
　　Disappearing
　　　On Glastonbury Mountain,

Climbing Wantastiquet
　Abenaki Mountain,
　　Where the rivers converge.

From Stratton Tower,
　Seeing the living land
　　From many directions,
　　　A panorama
　　　　Radiant in fortune-telling winds,
　　　　　Root-bound
　　　　　　In the floating world,
　　　　　　　Hiking through the pine trees'
　　　　　　　　Music of dreams,

There will never be anyone
  Like Malonta and Don Hugo,
    Welcoming hikers,
      Where the Long Trail
        And the Appalachian Trail
          Come together in praise,

Blessed by solitude
  And story,
    In the infinite fire of joy,

Crows laughing on The Tower of Hope
  Ruby-throated hummingbirds, brightly glowing.

TELLURIC:
ON MOUNTAIN ROAD

The Portal to the Otters
-Adelaide Scully Porter

For Hugh and Jeanne

Painting the heated ash of solitude,
 The red sun of Equinox,
   Welcoming the mystery,
Deep listening
  On the mountain path
    To the bear corridor
      That deepens the soul,
Listening to ululating coyote's
  At the break of day.

Who dreams the wind?
  Who dreams the world's tears?
    At the portal of the otters,
      The window to the caves.

WIND OF SOULS
For Hugh and Jeanne

Bloodstar of good fortune
　Sleepwalking through the open world
　　Where fire-birds
　　　Torque the tides,
　　　　Singing the heart of trees.

Fireflies, like stars, pierce
　The tears of the new sun.
　　Ravens circle the dead
　　　Turning towards the azure sky.
　　　　Mockingbirds
　　　　　Shapeshifting mountain ash,
　　　　　Sing beyond time.

FIRETOWER

For Kira

My daughter's raven cries
   Pierce the burnt wind
      As owls cry into the moonlit night
         Praying for rain.

Summer shimmers
   Like the blown glass of dead stars,
      Bioluminescent on the mountain path,
         As fireflies spark
            The glow of our minds
               Sucking the dirt candy
                  Of collective memory,
                     Our phosphorescence
                        Whirling out of time.

Riding through the amusement park's
   Scary rides
      With my eyes closed
         In dreams,
We dance together
   In the sacred trees
      Around the firetower,
         At the center of the world.

DAWN

Laughing,
  We return to mountain birds,
    Listening to
      The soul music of forgetting,
        With gratitude
          Seeded by time.

Lost on the mountain path
  Walking the inner music
    To the center of the world

Sometimes
  Truth-telling
    Hurts the Beloved friend,
      Better to be still
        In the night
          Speaking the blessings of renewal
            At dawn.

IRIDESCENCE:
PAINT LIKE A WOLF

For Frank Anthony

You call me the Black Pearl,
  But you are the Black Pearl,
    Our Black Pearl of inspiration and
      Artistry,
        Our I-Thou of reverence and story,
        Our jewel of ancestral song.

Your paintings mapping
  The Buffalo of Delaware County
    Dance with History's sun,

Zig-zagging with gratitude,
  As your stories unfold,
    "Paint like a wolf."

You, who are African, Spanish,
  Seminole, and a Jew,
    Know the meaning of Tribes,
      And what they mean to all of us,
        Fighting for unity's prayer
          Of pride and song.

FRIENDSHIP'S HEARTBEAT:
FADO OF EARTH AND SKY
FIRE AND WIND

For Gerald McBride

And if you were not
By my side,
There would be no fado,
Nor fadistas, like I am.

-Ana Moura

I
What hope is restored by
  Cordillera beauty of earth and sky,
    Deep listening to Neruda's spirit
      Burning through honeysuckle sulfur
        On Machu Picchu's mountain path,
          With your song that
            Deepens the night.

Haunting *Fado's*
  Rain of bees,
    "Desfado",
      Sweet song of sadness
        Singing the soul's
          Ash of solitude,
            Blessed by the light of dreams,

        "And if you were not
          By my side,
            There would be no *fado*,
              Nor *fadistas*, like I am.

Friendship's heartbeat
  In the green night,
    Listening to Sephardic songs,
      Of Gal Tamir,
        With mountain birds,
          Calling your name.

II

Listening to your violin's tears,
  Soul-brother of New Mexico's
    Fire and earth,

Listening to your
  Red-throated hummingbird heart beating
    Andalusian dream songs,
      In the dark branches,

Listening to your violin pulsing
  In the honeycomb hive,
    Center of the world

        "And if you were not
          By my side,
            There would be no *fado*,
              Nor fadistas, like I am."

FRIENDSHIP
For Gerald McBride

Songbirds spark
  Sandia winds
    Circling
      Your Berdache
        Dark pulse,
          High desert
            Pathway
              To the heart.

THE ARCHEOLOGY OF THE SOUL
For Barbara Clark

Every Angel Is Terrible
-Rilke

Your archeology of the soul,
  Crying out against tyranny
    Under the stars,

Your transcendent lyricism,
  Thundering through history,
    Shattering stars,

Your poetry's storytelling pulse,
  Transforming winter cold into gold,
    The infinite strangeness
      Mapping the wind's migration
        In the Book of Mysteries,

Your poetry
  Deep, like the rivers of life,
    Rising and falling
    In night winds,
      With Rilke's cries
        To the angels
          Evoking Rilke's Duino Elegies
          "Who if I cried out
            Would hear me amongst
              The angelic orders?"

Listening to the symbolic powers
  Singeing your world of despair,
    Yearning for freedom.

The Movie At The Back of Your Mind
   Singing a love song
     To Sor Juana Inés de la Cruz
      "Who lived too early
        To openly love women"

Your extravagantly resonant
   Incandescence
     Facing the sea,
       Shatters the mystery of incendiary dreams,
        Driving your archeology of the soul.

THE TABLETS OF DESTINY

Songpoems aflame
  In the winds and rain
    Who will carry our hope over the waters?

Meditating on
  Who we were
    And what we are becoming.

Who will carry the hidden sacred
  Honoring Earth's beauty
    Back to the well of love

      Knowing
        The difference between what we want
          And what destiny wants from us?

In the ghazal of friendship
  We take our friendship vows. . .
    Who are we now?

CLARITY

For Claire Longtin North (La Luna)

With clarity of blue winds
  Spiraling the earth with song
    Believing
       In your storytelling pulse
        Of devotion and humor,
         Praying for renewal,
          The mystery under
           The full cold winter moon,
            The shimmer of mountain ash,

As we lean into poetry that unites
  Us in Peace,
Tearing Poetry
  From The Book of Dreams,
    Illuminating your Irish ancestry,
    Radiant with pride,
      The moon's incandescence,
       With you rubbing holy oil
      On the Tree of Life.

May the blessings and mysteries
  Of the season,
    Shine through us,

May the dream sacraments
  Of deep winter
    Light our way.

SUN MAD
For Ester Hernandez

In Migrant dreams,
   The dead rise up like Calaveras,
      Sun Mad in pesticides,
         Raisins, "unnaturally grown with
            Insecticides herbicides, fungicides,"
               As skeletons dance
                  Through fields of song,
                     With Cesar Chavez and Dolores Huerta,
                        Rooted in the history of displacement.

The dead rise up
   In migrant winds,
      Poised on tender earth,
         "La Lucha Continua,"
            Struggling for farmworker's rights,

Crying for affirmation and resistance,
   From the House of Song,
      As the mountains
         Rise up like Yaqui angels
            Sparking the heat of dawn.

OUR LADY OF GUADALUPE

For Yolanda López

Our Lady of Guadalupe
  With your cloak of stars,
    Emerging from your Sunday shell,
     Running with a healing snake,
      Mujer Chicana,
       Devoted to Freedom's song,

Your painted icon,
  Leaping over the red carpet angel,
   Celebrating your liberation,
    Your enduring spirit,
     Your ancestral strength,
      Your radiant light.

THE CALL OF DEATH:
THE CALL OF LIFE
For Judith Repetti

After viewing The Diego Rivera murals
  At The Palace of Fine Arts
    In Mexico City.
      We drove the mountain pass
        To Orizaba's majestic beauty,

"G-d, put wings on this car,"
  We sang to the winds,
    As a truck came towards us
      On a narrow one lane
        Passageway over a cliff,
          Crows and ravens
            Circling us from above.

"Put wings on this car"
  We murmured,
    As we flew
      Over the truck,
        Ignoring the call to death,
          Landing safely at
            Pico de Orizaba's purple corn,
              At the entranceway,
                Embracing our luck.

TIME

> *For the Maya,*
> *Time was born and had a name,*
> *When the sky didn't exist,*
> *And the earth had not yet awakened.*
> *-Eduardo Galeano*

Guatemala's bees burst through
  The fifth sun,
    Sweet honey in the heart,
      The heart-womb of love,
        The honeysuckle sulfur
          Of burnt clay.

The Maya believe
  On the 400th day,
    The soul is freed
      From the body's restraints,

To the eye of the spiral
  We fly,
    From the luminous fires of life,
      We return.

WHERE PEOPLE ARE TREES

For Steve Minkin

> *At a certain point, poetry asks you*
> *Why you are here,*
> *How much are you prepared to give up,*
> *How much are you willing to lose?*
> *-Steve Minkin*

Rising up the spine of the land
  In Chiapas, Mexico
    Where people are trees,
      Imagining a protective canopy for refugees,

Tears of collective memory
  Well up as beauty
    Deepens the forest's
      Shadows at dawn.

Children selling vanilla,
  At the foot of mountains
    Speak to me
      From the roots of song,
            Holding passion flowers'
              Silver sage and piñon,

Ex-votos and milagros,
  Blinded by a miracle,
    Pulse with dread,
      As night,
        Pierced by milk thistle and mesquite,
          Drips poetry, from the deep sulphured sap,
            You ask,
              "How much are you prepared to give up?"
              "How much are you willing to lose?"

HARLEM

Dreams of wind
  Reflected in the child's broken mirror,
    Ambulances at Grants' Project
      On LaSalle
        Follow the smell of burning.

An air plane
  Flying a banner on 125th Street
    And Broadway
      Skywrites, "Never Again"
        Crows form a revenant of prayer,
          Hassids, handing out pamphlets,
            Ask if we are Jews.
              Moving passed their baby carriages
                Without sharing our ancestral pride,
                  Our roots,
                    The mystery of our open souls.

BELIEF

For Gerald McBride

Arroyo of sand-swept dunes,
  Night of the jack-rabbit's deepening.
    Hope for rain,
      Soul dance of the owl's
        Return from darkness,
          Lightning's circular desert
            Lost in time.

Remembering your Berdache cry
  Invoking the divine,
    "Say it as a prayer of belief,"
      Your violin
        Whirling in the Sandia's piñon pine.

THE TWILIGHT OF THE IGUANAS

Driving passed Iguanas
  On the canals
    Off the Freeway passed Delray,
      Crows slow-dancing in the lilacs
        Mapping winds,

Old women from the
  Black-market cassino
    Dance with the dead,
      Feeding iguana's
        Under the incendiary sky,
          As we drive by.

LOXAHATCHEE WILDLIFE SANCTUARY,
Florida

The slash palm and the saw palmetto.
Anhinga's like sphinx
Move like Angels across the sky,
Velvet ants in their round dance
Bend on cypress knees,
As the moons of the fingernails rise.

DREAMS IN THE TIME OF COVID

Green mountain grackles
  Quarantine
    On our dirt road,
      In the mineral twilight
        Surrounding the hemlock and pines,
          The sulphur of dead bees,
            The ache of mountain ash.

We witness
  The beauty of dawn
    As ululating coyotes
      Spiral the earth with song,
        Crows with singed wings
          Fly
            As we walk by.

EVERGREEN
For Bob

Standing under the canopy of trees,
  Grounded by the roots of the world,
    Believing in the power of witness,
      Under the balsam and pines.

  Under the azure of trees.
    The red fox dreams of a bus ticket home,
      Reaching for the
          Ghazal of the horned- owls
            Mountain heart,
              Friend of poetry and music,
                Singing the barred owl's soul.

The silver sky horse
  Gallops through fireflies,
    In the starry night.
      We watch the mother hummingbird
        Teach her babies to lick pollen
          Raising the sparks to dawn.
            The wind brings me back to you,
              Singing a love song.

WAFFLE CHILD

I was called "The waffle child of imperfection,"
  My delicious burnt-edges delighting all.
    The waffles would get better
      As the iron got hotter.
        My sisters, reaching another level of perfection,
          Under the stars.

I learned to live with my imperfections,
  Lifting me up,
    Guiding me to become
      The woman I am,
        Shining my light
          From the opalescent dark.

KEW GARDEN HILLS

We lived by the powers of our imagination,
  Roses bloomed outside our
    Garden apartment in Queens.
     Friends of the fortuneteller
      Surrounded us,
       In operatic dreams.

Arthur, chewing garlic,
  Picked up trash
   With a pointed stick.

Marsha's parents
  Cursed each other on
   Their way to work.

The wind pushed our swings
  In the alchemy of delight.
   Edith painted our portraits
    In the night's
     Shadow and light.

SONGLINES 2:
DESERT SOUL

You follow earth migrations
  On your ancestral path,
    Through Alice Springs'
      Exiled song,
        Mining opals
          At Coober Pedy's
            Deep mineral silence,
          In the night.

You follow
  High desert music's
    Alcheringa of burning sand,
      Black tourmaline
        In the shadows of
          Uluru's sacred sight.

        Shine your light
          Shattering the road of life's
            Desert sun.

WHALE STATION

Akureri, Iceland

We smelled the whale mothers
  Slaughtered
    At the whale station
      On the planks
        Of dark earth,

The great whale mothers
  In the firewind's
    Blood and smoke,
      In the death of winter's dark.

NIGHT WALKING UNDER
THE BLUE MOON'S SINGING WIND
West Wardsboro, Vermont

Listening to the dead sing
  In the dark branches,
    "A Love Supreme,"
      Rising star,
        Luminous
          At the center of the world.

DISSONANCE

Caterpillars in their gossamer tent
  Criss-cross the earth's mystery,
    Butterflies rising to the piano bar
      Sing "Metamorphosis,"
        As we sip wine,
          Stringing the blue beads of time.

CRY

For Blue Monk
(1917-1982)

And for Brian Fitzpatrick

Thelonious Monk's zig-zagging
  Dissonant mystery
    Rising up from the
      Violent death streets,
        Sounds his lost chord to freedom,

Humming "Round Midnight's"
  Twelve bar blues,
    Improvising bebop's "Live in Paris,"
      Lapis Jazz,
        Fireflies on the sidewalk,
          Spark angels imprisoned with strangers,
            "Straight, No Chaser,"
              Running the light,

As the hyacinth fire
  Gash of iridescence
    Pierces the night.

NIGHT HOPE:
IN TABLETS LOST IN STORMS

Migration's flame shatters
  The River G-d
    While crossing over
      The Border's Soul.

The mystery of Poetry
  Revealed
    At the mouth of the river's bend,
      Seeks the open world.

Suddenly, a cry for help,
  As we move from the terror of misfortune,
    Breaking open the winds
      That burnish stars.

LAPIS JAZZ
For Thelonius Monk,
(October, 1917-February, 1982)

We lean into the Blues
  With your broken mirror
    On the desert floor,
      Painting arroyo dream-sands,
        Timeless,
          That kiss you,
            As añil de muerto sunflowers
            Bend towards
            Your love,
              Your glass-star incandescence,
              Thelonius,
                Falling. Falling.

Thunderbirds fly into the sun,
  Into the sweet gum, liquid amber,
    Black notes of Lapis Jazz,
      "Round Midnight"
        Mysterious
          As a heartbreat.

THE ALCHEMY OF UNKNOWING
For Wayne Shorter (1933-2023)

Your tenor sax harmonics
  Of blue jazz
    Deepens bebop trance,
      Dark honey
        In the fusion of dance,

The Alchemy of Unknowing
  "Nefertiti"
    "My most sprung-from me,
      All in one piece,
        Experience of music writing,
          Like someone
            Recalling a trance"

Eternal,
  With Art Blakey's Jazz Messengers,
    Aflame,
      And Miles Davis'
        "Jazz washes away the dust of everyday life,"
          Call and Response,
            Your *"Speak No Evil,"*
              With Horace Silver's *"Song For My Father,"*
            In the early days,
                Improvising Joy and Love.

Newark follows you,
  Risking the impossible,
  Polishing your horn
    Free in
      "Sakeena's Vision,"
        Your *'House of Jade',*
          "Endangered Species"
            Floating out of time.

Your deep - song beauty,
Blessing the moon,
Spiral grace of fire,
Hugging the earth,
Salting the world's soul,
The lightning's wing.

HOMECOMING

The Haitian doorman who speaks five languages,
  Waits for his children to welcome him home
    To Port-au-Prince after
      Aristide was deposed.

Haiti's loas welcome him
  As he greets his family
    Crying out for Justice and Love.

SHATTERED

What was I looking for
    Talking trash with the angels,
        As countries burned?

In the horror of witness
    Singing of Hope and Loss

"*Injustice anywhere is a threat to justice*
Everywhere. We are caught in an
Inescapable network of mutuality, tied in
A single garment of destiny. Whatever
Affects one directly, affects all indirectly."
-Dr Martin Luther King

"*O, olive brothers,*
I ask for your forgiveness,
I ask for your forgiveness:"
-Mahmoud Darwish

"*Tell me what it looks like when the*
olive groves have burned,
And mist rolls in at dawn over
Charred earth and sifts between
Skeletal branches.It may take this
Scorching to make peace on earth.

The lost pyres have petered out.
If bones stick to ash, they are barely
distinguishable from roots. In the empty
graves,among twisted ghostly forms,
We dreamed justice was done."
-Rosanna Warren

"*I have been true to the principles of*
nonviolence,developing a stronger and
stronger aversion to the ideologies of
the far right and the far left and a
deeper sense of rage and sorrow over the sorrow they
continue to produce all over the world."
-Joan Baez

FRAGMENTS OF FRAGMENTS
SHARDS OF SHARDS 2

We fall into wordlessness
  Crying out
    For those
      Living the pain

Israelis and Palestinians
  Perished in the murders.

We cry out communally
  For a cease-fire
    To stop the killing

We cry out communally
  To stop the pain.

OCTOBER 7
THE SHATTERED STARS

Our Lost Tribe
  Shatters stars
    From the burning sands
      Of displacement

Our tribe of tears
  Sparks a siege
    In the gash of centuries

      The Ten Sefirot
        Shatters into
          The unspeakable
          The unsayable

THE RAPTURE OF STORY

In my family's Workman's Circle
  Socialist,
    I Gubener Ind Ben
      Ancestral graveyard
        At Mount Hebron cemetery
          In Queens

Where generations of musicians,
  Magicians and vaudevillians
    Were put to rest
      In the arms of perpetual care.

Workman Circle Jews
  Bought these plots
    When they arrived
      Penniless to New York City
        From Minsk and Tansk

Fleeing pogroms,
  Their burial plots came first,
    Falling
      Into the rapture of story.

PRAYER OF THE HEART

For Hisham Avartani
Kinnan Abdel Hammid,
Tahseed Amed

Wearing *keffiyehs* while walking here,
  On Prospect Street in Burlington,
    Shot and injured
      Walking together with joy in your hearts
       While visiting a grandma
      On Thanksgiving day,

Your grandmother trembles
  Amidst the gunshots
    Hoping for a cease-fire,
      The ever-lastingness of belief,
      Healing and prayer.

REMEMBERING THE NIGHT
OF THE DEAD'S WHITE SHROUD

Night owls know the smell of death in the world
  Drinking from the Sea of Tears
    Remembering the Night of the Dead's white shroud,
    The shrouded dark,
      The rubble wounds,
        Wind-ash
          Born in the shadow of war.

Tell me the nights of remembering
  The path of destruction,
    The torque of atrocity,
      Violence begetting more violence,
        Envisioning a Just and Lasting Peace.

      "And now the olive trees are sleeping"*
        Let us mourn together.

* Song by Judeo-Spanish singer songwriter Yasmin Levy

NEW SONG

Why, in dreams,
　Crossing The Sea of Reeds.
　　We cross the Sea of Dangers
　　　Passing the tunnels
　　　　Hamas has buried
　　　　　In the darkness.

　Exiled from our souls,
　　Listening to Yom Yabasha ,
　　　A Passover Song
　　　　Created from a poem by
　　　　The twelfth century Sephardic poet,
　　　　　Yehuda Halevi

　　　"The day the depths
　　　　Turned to dry land"
　　　　　Played on the violin and oud,

At The Sea of Reeds,
　Exiled from our souls,
　　We cross the Sea of Dangers
　　　Longing for a cease-fire
　　　　And a return of hostages,
　　　　　Leaving our longing for Peace
　　　　　In the dust of days to come.

TWILIGHT

Listening to orphans cry out
  In the world's sorrow
    Bending the arc's soul,

As a river of Palestinians flee
  The safe zone,
And Israelis under a black sun
  Wait for hostages to come home,

There's no safe place in Gaza,
  Lost in the burnt ruins
    In the winds of war,
      Waiting for a cease-fire
        To take place in Doha.

Time trembles through
  The blood of centuries,
    The hope of ancient mothers
      Keeping the peace
        Under the olive trees.

Leaflets of warning
  Fall on Rafa,
    Exiling Palestinians
      Once again
        From their burned out homes.

As the dead and the living conjoin,
  Praying for dignity,
    In the days to come.

LOST

Children in lost worlds
  Rake shards in orphan winds.

The one-eyed crow in Gaza
  Screes the war-torn land
    As the moon breaks open.

LAMENTATION

Exiled poet speak, in your century
What do you see?
-Odysseus Elytes

From our soul house of ancestral pain
  We bless the roots of trees,
     Listening to the storm of
        Broken souls
           Predicting the fractured sacred.

Friends cry out
  In the medicine winds
     From their sanctuaries of life.

     Fleet-footed as a deer
        We praise the forest's horn-moon
           Planting the black seeds of mourning.

THE BATTAN DEATH MARCH

For Myrrl W. McBride
Who survived The Bataan Death March
And for Gerald McBride

When the names were called out from
  The Bataan Death March,
    Tar and blood, the violent heat
      Scorched your forehead
        At the jungle's edge,
          The blue smoke of dead trees
            And the lilac smoke of corpses
          Seeped into you.

You were twenty years old
  When the winds came in
    Like flying glass
      Piercing your soul.

Who, coming out of torment
  Hears the night's memory of hunger
    Closing the eyes of the dead?
      As your heart threw off it's torque of tears,
        Scavenging for star anise and dorian seeds
        To sustain your friends
        Dying of starvation,
        Risking it all.

         Take me to another place
         Of sacred tenderness
          Reaching for the abyss,
            Away from the destitution of time
          In the open.

Bring me home
　　To the tents of music
　　　　Where the crying never ends

FOR THE CHILDREN IN ATLANTA

Pero el llanto es un pero immenso,
el llanto es un angel immenso,
El llanto es un violin inmenso,
La lágrima amordazan al viento,
Y no se oye otra cosa que el llanto.

> *But the weeping is an immense dog,*
> *the weeping is an immense angel,*
> *the weeping is an immense violin,*
> *the tears muzzle the wind,*
> *nothing else is heard but the weeping.*
> *-Federico Garcia Lorca*

Fire agate cracking open in Atlanta   Fire imprisoned in stone,
Our mothers can't sleep, our fathers can't sleep,
Mad beast hanging in the shadows is tearing out our hearts.

I caress you son,   my hands like fire-gourds reaching out,
I call to you, son   my song like a shadow striking dust,
I cry to you love,   the blood in my deep song burst to tears,

I plant black roses, here
Where the earth aches for her children,

Y no se oye otra cosa que el llanto,
Nothing else is heard but the weeping.

AND HE KEPT ON SINGING

For Victor Jara
Here I Remain To Sing Back The Ghosts

Deep in the night you sing your intricacies
  Of passion
    Aqui Me Quedo
      Your lava voice trickling blood
        From an open wound,

Pluck the anguish ripe from darkness
  Where the soul burns like cactus
    In desert arenas

And they sing solidarity, The full moon
  Throbbing copper.
And they sang like rivers breaking open
  From the blood wounds
    Of your hands.

BARAYE* (BECAUSE)

For Persian Composer, Singer-Songwriter,
-Shervan Hajipour

Tell me how you lived your dream in some Place
And I'll tell you who you are.
-Fady Joudah

Listening to your heartbeat arabesque
  "For Peace and Serenity,"
    "For Women, Life, and Freedom,"
      Imprisoned for singing Freedom's song.

Listening to Baraye's black butterflies return
   Incantation's promise,
     Glass beads in freedom's wind,
       Healing trauma's scars
         Heart wisdom of
           Earth's beauty
             Under Persian stars.

Fragments of dreams
  Shelter
    Indigo seeds of longing,
      Under the crescent moon.

Shards of the divine
  Shadow the mirror of time,
    In the protest-prayers of world song,
      When will this war on culture and Women's Right's end?

*Baraye was inspired by the brutal death of a 22-year-old Iranian woman Mahisa Amini,
September 16th, 2022

AFTER GREAT SORROW

Abandoning everything, take refuge in me
-Daniel Simko

After this long winter suicide,
  The giving, and the taking of life,
    Hornets in cupped hands
      Come home to haunt you,
        The burnt lilac soot lingers
          In the great sorrow
            As hyacinth fire settles in
              Listening to the soul of birds
            In mother winds.

Your grandma's black tablecloths
  Flow with roses,
    Amongst the forest pines.
    Friends take their place
      At the night feast
        Of charred potatoes and beets,
        Root vegetables
          To celebrate the earth's turning,
          The moon's sacred smoke
          Diaphanous under
          Shattered glass.

Would she have burned you
  As the fire wrapped itself with bees,
    As crows cried in grief,
      "Abandoning everything
      Take refuge in me."

"BESIEGE YOUR SIEGE"
-Mahmoud Darwish

For Mahmoud Darwish (1941-2008)

When will Peace open her doors to the doves?
-Mahmoud Darwish

From the hive of dispossession,
    The poetry of resistance,
        Besieged in Lebanon's heart,

 Whirl the right palm upwards
   And the dance begins,
     Whirl the shadow dance through time,
       Return the sparks to humankind.

Encountering
   The Cedars of Lebanon's shadow breath,
     The checkpoints of borders,
       The strangers Salaam,

        "Am I another you,
          And you another I"

         'Then let's be kind"

What will we do with our fear?
   Lilacs in the exiled ash of forgetting,
     Muwashahs in Palestine,
       Dispossessed in the changing world.

"BESIEGE YOUR SIEGE" 2

For the essayist and poet
-Mosab Abu Toha

Detained and beaten
  By Israeli Defense Forces
    At the Rafa Crossing
      Between Gaza and Egypt
        Rescued by pressure
          From the World's literary community,

Your book of poems,
  Things You May Find
    Hidden In My Ear

Haunts us
  With its heartbreaking
    Lived experience
      Of being alive
        In Gaza

With its shrapnel and smoke bombs,
  Infused with strawberry water
    And morning dew,
      It's refugee ruins,
        It's Palestinian pride,
          Checkpoint to checkpoint,
            Prayer to prayer.

How the wind stirs you
  With hope,
    As you write

"Hope is a difficult word for Palestinians.
It is not something that
Others gives us but, something
We must cultivate and care for
On our own.
We have to help grow hope."*

*Excerpt in The New Yorker, January - March, 2023.

BEHEMOTH

"When are we in danger?"
"When are we not in danger?"
-Carol Heffer

With your clawed feet
 Speaking in the ruins of time
  Under long-haired stars
   Of the ancient moon,

Your crooked teeth
 In the dark night
  Of fallen angels
   Under the terebinth
    Tree of berries and fire
     Biting the hand of G-d,

Crawling through the blood of the land,
 Oligarch,
  Stripping our rights away
   Incendiary
    Growling from the asylum's rack
     As we fight back,

LEVIATHAN

Leviathan at the cusp of catastrophe,
  Shape-shifting sea-serpent
    Shedding her skin,
      Chimera,
        Swimming under the crescent moon's rising tide,

Dead bees destroying ash caves
  With burning wings,

Spirit-bearing
  Bleeding women in
    Wrapped tunnels
      Basking with grandma whales
       Washed up on the shore,

The mother-blood of dolphins,
  Drunk with castor oil,
    Dragged to earth,
      Warming to dragon birth.

AMERICA, THE UNBEAUTIFUL

A cacophony of crows
  Closes in on us
    Rotting our mother-tongue,

The beauty of bloodroot
  Beckons us,
    Walking through the cemetery of strangers,
      The blood of sumac
        Staining our legs,

Walking through corn fields
  Of spacious sky's
    Purple mountains majesty,
      Hearing the piercing cry
        "Rite of Asylum: Asylum's Rite"

The earth closing in
  As ICE picks up
    Students on the street,
      America the Unbeautiful seizes the democratic free,
        Crows cry
          "Take refuge in me."

PEACE BE WITH YOU
For Myra Barovick (1937-2022)*

The first shovel of dirt on your coffin
  Is for reluctance,
    The second shovel of dirt
      Over your coffin
        Is for acceptance.

At Peace in your purple shroud,
  The dead and the living surround you,
    Palms up, grieving your loss,
      The Malach Hamovis,
        The Angel of Death,
          Blesses you,
            In the cemetery of dreams,
              The wind blowing through us.

*At the Holy Hebrew Society Cemetery in South Berlington, Vermont.

ANCESTRAL 2

Dreaming the lost writing on turtle shells
Black sands of memory,
White-scrolled *Shema* of silver mezuzah's
Eye-dazzling wisdom
Blanketing the lost questions,
  Involuting,
    Turning back and forth upon themselves,
Zim-zum The letting free
Under the green canopy
Of the forest's soul.

In a time of no shadow,
Our grandparents cry out
From a field of crows.

ELDERS

Grateful for your wisdom,
　As our bodies deceive us,
　　Are we wise about our loss?

It's the hidden sparks
　That thunder to the core,

　　A quiet rain,
　　　A wind chime.

NIGHT PSALM RADIANCE

For Yasmin Levy
  Israeli singer-songwriter of Judeo -Spanish music.

Night restores fragments of
  Broken-hearted melodies,
    Heart-womb of the angel's longing,
      Singing,
        "Una Noche Mas,"
          "And now the olive trees are weeping"
          "Olvidate de mi"
            "Forget me"

Fireflies lost in mystery
  Dream the dark-light
    Honey of redemption,
      Seeking honey in sand,

Singing the rising and falling of grief,
  Blessed by the light of dreams,
    Illumined by sky,
      From the pool of lamentation,
        Where all the tears reside,

        Light the temple lamps
          Welcoming the mystery.

LICKING SCARLET

Just don't go listening to those
  Torch-holding Cassandra's
    Burning dreams
      Into the heart of fate,

Night visions' dissonant
  Thrum of angels
    Calling in the dead year.

Children sleepwalk through
  The riveting willows,
    The raven runes,
      Burning the roots of trees.

Let the winds augur
  The knot of blood
    In Queen Anne's lace,
      Oracle of lover's dreams
        Of enchantment
          And freedom's song.

DIRT CANDY

What was I looking for
  Talking trash with the angels
    While candles burned?

Children eat dirt candy
  Sent into the world
    With wooden sticks.

We play patient and doctor
  On Eileen's porch,
    After eating a pregnant woman's medicine
      Thrown into the trash bin.

I tell my mother
  "I was the patient"
    She tells me,
      "Next time, you be the doctor."

WHAT KIND OF COUNTRY IS THIS? 2

What kind of country is this
   Where people sign up
     To lose their health
       and well-being,
Where all our hard - fought rights
   Are crushed
     At the break of day?

FADO OF FATE

Fado of fate
  Branching night trees'
  Shrapnel and lace,
    Amber resins of tar,
    Raven-heart

FADO

Wasting away with love,
  Fado
Astonished by love,
   Recklessness be damned,
    Fado
Moonstruck
   Where peacocks sound like hinges,
    Fado
Who turns you 'round
   In the windy street?
   Fado
Why don't you love me?
   Fado
Draw your fear unto me
   Fleet-footed as a dear
    Fado

Listening to Amália Rodriguez's
  Barco Negro,
   Música do Portugal
    My vision
     Blinded by tears

"You are in the wind
  Which spreads sand on the glass,"
"You are in the water
   That sings into the dying fire"
"You are in the warmth of the nest
  From empty seabirds"
"You are forever with me,
   In my heart
    Fado

DESTINY

Everything I painted was
   Hidden away,
      As if in a war zone,

We were folding quesadillas,
   When the bedbugs took over
      Our bodies.

We listened to the music
   Of snowshoe hares.

We were rapidly aging
   But knew our wisdom
      Would drive our cares.

We opened to the force of destiny
   To destiny's winds.

THE LIVING EMBERS

Awake at dawn
So much yammering
And still
No way to break the silence.

ACKNOWLEDGEMENTS

"On Hearing Thunder," first published in *On Hearing Thunder*; blurbs by Joy Harjo, Rosanna Warren, Hilda Morley; North Star Press, St. Cloud, MN: 2004. Read at Wahru Cleveland's Memorial by Jeanne Flanigan, Oklahoma City, 2023; by Joyce Mauer at a celebration of Life ceremony, Columbus, Ohio, 2023; and by Lisa Ferraro at the National Women's Music Festival, 2023.

"And He Kept On Singing" for Victor Jara, *Rattle*, Cardinal Press, Tulsa, OK, 1982. Blurbs by Joy Harjo, introduction by Meridel Le Sueur.

"For The Children in Atlanta," First published as a broadside. Four Zoas Press, MA: *Rattle*, and Cardinal Press: Tulsa, Oklahoma in 1982 with an introduction by Meridel Le Sueur and blurb by Joy Harjo.

"When People Were Trees," For Steve Minken, "Poems About Town," Brattleboro, Vermont: 2024.

Poetry Reading for Write Action's Spotlight Reading, Latchis Theatre, Brattleboro Literary Festival, Brattleboro, Vermont: 2021, 2023.

Poetry Reading with Toni Ortner, Putney Library, Vermont, 2021, 2023.

Poets On The Street: Brattleboro, Vermont, 2021, 2022, 2023.

Poetry Reading, Temple Sinai, South Burlington, 2023.

In Memoriam, Poetry Reading, and painted "Dragon Scroll," exhibited, Revelation Gallery, Waverly Place, NYC, for the International Women's Salon in partnership with St. John's In The Village.

Mixed-Media Painted Scrolls, West Wardsboro Library, VT: 2023, 2024.
Mixed Media Painted Scrolls "Chez Nous," Wilmington, Vermont: 2023.

Mixed-Media Painted Scrolls, "The Singing of The Soul, Is The Nature of Art, Herself", Arthouse; exhibition and performance with musician Brian Fitzpatrick, Wilmington, Vermont: 2024.

ABOUT THE AUTHOR

Shattered is Terry Hauptman's eighth volume of poetry. She holds a Master's Degree in Poetry from The University of New Mexico, Albuquerque—where she studied with poet laureate, Joy Harjo—and a Ph.D in Interdisciplinary Arts from Ohio University. She reads her poetry rhapsodically and exhibits her luminous 5'x40' Songline Scrolls nationally. She has taught World Art, Poetry, and Ethnopoetics at several universities and workshops, most recently at Green Mountain College. She lives in Vermont with Robert and Kira.